Blossom Caught Fish

by Carlos Ash
illustrated by Nicole Rutten

Practice Decodable 78

McGraw Hill Education

Bothell, WA • Chicago, IL • Columbus, OH • New York, NY

MHEonline.com

Send all inquiries to:
McGraw-Hill Education
8787 Orion Place
Columbus, OH 43240

ISBN: 978-0-02-130710-4
MHID: 0-02-130710-5

Printed in the United States of America.

7 8 9 CTM 23

Mom and Pop had a daughter. Her name was Blossom. They thought she was sweet.

Mom and Pop brought Blossom by the river. They taught her to fish. Fishing was hard at first for Blossom.

Blossom didn't do as she was taught. She jumped into the river and splashed.

But soon Blossom caught a lot of fish. Mom and Pop felt proud. Then Mom and Pop grew older.

Mom and Pop did not fish. They bought fish in stores. Big Blossom did not know.

But Blossom found out.

"I ought to catch fish for Mom and Pop."

She did. Blossom was still sweet.